SHE KEPT GOING

Part 1

Dedicated to:

This book series is dedicated to my grandmother, the late D'orlyly "Cookie" Freeman and my grandfather, the late George Dupree. Without the supervision and coaching of these two people throughout my life as a child, I wouldn't be where I am today. Both was all about education and encouraging others to get through hard times. Continue to rest in heaven, both of you.

Acknowledgements

Thank you to my editor, MC Walker. Without you, I couldn't have made this dream come true of becoming an author of my own story. You did an awesome job!

Chapter One

July 4th, 1993

It sounded like fireworks on the Fourth of the July. There were no fireworks lighting up the night sky. My eyes opened wide as I could hear the sound of a loud explosion piercing my ear drums. Too afraid to move inside my twin bed I hurriedly pulled the covers over my eyes. I counted to ten slowly like my momma had told me to do when I had a bad dream.

Except this nightmare wasn't inside my head, it was a few feet outside my bedroom window. My heart began to race rapidly as the loud sounds became more frequent. Too afraid to move I began to cover my ears. I knew the noise outside my bedroom window wasn't fireworks. They were gunshots. Part of me wanted to run and look out the window and see what was happening. I knew momma wouldn't like that. She said to always mind my business and stay in a child's place. I listened sometime. As my floral print cover shielded my face and body, I couldn't help but wonder about my mom. I knew if I heard the gunshots she did too. My mouth was too dry to yell out for her and I didn't want to cause more trouble.

One gunshot woke me up.

Two gunshots caused me to almost pee myself.

Three gunshots caused me to crawl out of my bed and out my bedroom door.

I wasn't ready for what I was about to see on the living room. I couldn't believe my eyes. It was like I was inside of a scary movie and couldn't wake up. Tears began to fall from my eyes. I was scared at the sight of all the blood covering the floor and the sofa. I was crying because I saw my momma crying. She was holding Melvin inside her arms. He was moaning loudly as blood began to spill across his once pristine white shirt. I didn't know where he'd been shot. It was too much blood to see a bullet wound. I was too afraid to take a step closer. I began to cry loudly as everything began to unfold before my eyes.

She Kept Going Part 1 — Simmone Jones

I could hear my mom yelling for me to grab a towel. She cradled her lover inside her arms and prayed to God for a miracle. I felt helpless in that moment. I knew my mother needed me. There was nothing I could do to change the situation. Tears began to rush down my cheek as I trembled inside my pj's. The gun shots were gone. I was praying that this would not mean that Melvin wouldn't be gone too. I knew how much he meant to my mother's happiness and at times our family.

Suddenly the moans from Melvin got a little lower. It was like the pain had suddenly come to an end. My mother kept calling his name and screaming at the top of her lungs. She screamed so loud that I thought her soul had left her body. I covered my eyes and began rocking back and forth on the living room floor. It was the only thing I knew how to do in the middle of a crisis. I could feel my lips moving. Nothing was coming out on the other end. My heart was beating rapidly inside my chest that I thought I was going to pass out.

Within a matter of minutes, the ambulance truck arrives, and two older white men rush inside our tiny house. They push my mom out of the way and start attending to Melvin needs. I don't know how my mom got up from the floor. Every time I looked at her it looked as if a part of her soul was beginning to die by the second. My mother continued to scream. The police officers rushed inside the living room and escorted me and my mom into the back room. My mom put up a big fight because she didn't want to miss anything. No matter how much she cried the police officers wouldn't allow us back inside the living room.

I reached for my mom's hand as the police officer guarded the door.

"It's going to be okay mom." I whispered softly.

She looked back at me with fear in her glossy brown eyes. Gone was the face that kissed me goodnight on my cheek. Replaced by fear and anxiety my mom had aged in one night by ten years. Something inside of me wanted to comfort and protect her like she'd done me. But I didn't feel equipped enough to handle the level of the magnitude of the burden on her shoulders. I just sat next to my mom and held her hand.

It seemed like it took forever. The cop monitoring us tapped my mom on her shoulder and said, "He's going to make it. Do you need a ride to the hospital?"

Without question, my mom nodded her head and finally released a deep breath.

Chapter Two

The paramedics escorted my mom into the back of the ambulance. The bright red and blue lights began to hurt my eyes. There were police officers everywhere and cars all over the yard. Everyone was talking so fast that I could barely understand. I was too afraid to move. When my mother walked out the front door, she didn't look back at me. It was like a part of her had left inside the ambulance with Melvin already and we were looking at her shell. The police officers began taking photographs of the crime scene. The sight of the blood terrified me. There was so much blood everywhere I didn't know how to feel on the inside.

"Do you have someone we can call?' A voice asked me.

I looked up with tears in my eyes. Words would not come out of my mouth no matter how hard I tried to speak.

"What's your name sweetheart?" A blonde-haired blue eyes woman asked on one knee. She scribbled in her notebook as she examined me closely with her eyes. She just kept asking me question after question as the tears began to stream more frequently down my face.

'I want my momma." I mumbled through my tears.

The young woman just looked at me like I was just another thing on her to do list. She made more lines in her notebook and nodded her head towards me. I closed my eyes hoping that the tears would stop falling down my cheek. I wanted to be a big girl in the moment. But I was more scared than I'd ever been in my entire life.

She Kept Going Part 1   Simmone Jones

"I'm going to take you with me for the night." The young woman assured me briefly.

I opened my eyes to discover Lorraine walking in the front door like a hurricane. She snatches me by my arm and pulls me out the front door. Before I could say anything, you toss me into the backseat of her car and buckle my seatbelt. She heads back inside the house to grab my baby sister. I don't know if the police feared Lorraine or if they just didn't care what happened to us. No one seemed to stop us from leaving the house. Once we were inside the car safely,

Lorraine turned on the radio and began to pull out of the yard.

"I don't trust any white folks with black children." She mumbled.

Within a matter of minutes, we were heading down a dark road. The backseat window was down. The cool breeze washed my tears away. I reached for my baby sister hand and closed my eyes. For the first time that night, I felt safe.

She Kept Going Part 1					Simmone Jones

Chapter Three

As soon as we walked inside the hospital, I could feel my feet get heavier. My breathing began to slow down and my heart began to speed up. I hated hospitals! Everything about them made me nervous and frightened me to death. I remember when my momma cut her hand in the kitchen one night with a knife accidentally. Blood was everywhere. The sight of the blood made me queasy and nervous. I was too afraid to step into the kitchen for days. I tried not to think about all the blood in the hospital. I wanted to get to my mom as soon as possible. I needed to know that she was alright.

We were inside the elevator when Lorraine looked down at me and said,

"Jolene, I need you to be a big girl for your momma and sister, you understand?" I could tell by the sound in Lorraine's voice that she was serious. She hadn't said much during the car ride to the hospital. That was unusual for Lorraine. I nod my head yes because I knew that was what she wanted me to say. On the inside her nerves and mini pep talk wasn't helpful at all. Lorraine altered hips as she carried my baby sister through the hospital hallways. My baby sister rested her head on Lorraine's shoulder and wrapped her arm around her neck. She was tired and so was I.

I held onto Lorraine's hand as we walked down the hallway passing occupied rooms of sick and wounded people. Lorraine just looked down at me and said, "Everything is going to be alright". She mumbled frequently. I believe she was trying to convince herself more than me.

When I saw my mom for the first time since leaving the house, she looked much worse. I ran towards her like a bird in a sky. Her eyes widen as she opened her arms and greeted me with her round belly. Her eyes were blood shot red and swollen. She planted a kiss on my cheek, and I could feel the moistness from her face that her tears were fresh. She hugged me tightly and whispered, "Don't be scarred Jolene."

"I'm not." I whispered.

I could feel my tears coming up once more as I wrapped my arms tightly around my mom's neck. My mom began to rub my back and I could feel the intense burden on her back. Lorraine held on to my baby sister as she slept peacefully on her shoulders.

"What are the doctors saying?" Lorraine whispered.

I sat in the middle between them with my arms inside my shirt for warmth. I rested my head on my thin legs. We were sitting in the waiting room with two other people. We all looked nervous and hopeful for some good news. Out of all of us my mom looked the worst. She frequently ran her fingers through her hair and tapped her foot against the floor. Her blood-stained shirt had been replaced with a hospital gown and hospital jacket. I wanted to comfort my mom in this moment. But I felt powerless to do anything. I just sat next to her to relieve her stress.

"They haven't said anything since we got here." My mom replied.

"He's going to be fine, I bet." Lorraine reassured.

I didn't know who or what to believe. Another thirty to forty-five minutes went by before the doctors appeared. As soon as they entered the waiting room my mom walked over to them for an update. I couldn't hear a word that they were saying. I could just hear the sound of praise coming from my mom's mouth. She turned around and urged Lorraine and I to come over towards her with the doctors.

The doctors began to talk more, and I didn't understand anything. I just wrapped my arm around my mother's leg as she rubbed my head softly. Within a matter of minutes my mom's tears had been replaced with a toothy grin. For the first time that night we all smiled.

We were escorted to a different hallway. I could hear the sounds of moaning and the buzz of machines. I squeezed my mom's hand as she walked rapidly towards Melvin's room. I looked down at the floor because I didn't know what to expect when we would walk inside the hospital room. As soon as we arrived at Melvin room door I froze in time. I was afraid to go inside. I didn't want to see Melvin with tubes and machines attached to him. I wanted to black out and pretend like this moment wasn't happening to me or my mom.

"Mom? I'm scared." I cried.

My mom bent down on one knee and said, "It's okay Jolene, and we're all a little scarred. But, right now Melvin needs to know that we're here and we love him. We want him to get better, right?'

I nodded my head yes as tears began to cover my face. I could feel my hands trembling as more tears began to flow from my eyes. I nodded my head yes. But my feet would not allow me to enter Melvin's room.

"I can't…. I can't go in there…I can't". I cried.

My mom wrapped her arms around me. She held me so tightly that I could hardly breathe. I could feel her hands rubbing against my back. She whispered inside my ear. I couldn't hear the words too clearly because it felt like my heart was going to jump outside my chest.

Lorraine urged my mom to go inside Melvin's room and she'd stay outside to watch me. My mom kissed my cheek and promised me that she would be right back. She disappeared inside Melvin's room and closed the door behind her quietly. Within a matter of minutes, I could hear her screams like from earlier that night. I looked over at Lorraine and saw fear cover her once peaceful face. Within a matter of seconds, she ran inside the hospital room to comfort my mom. I sat in the hospital hallway crying nervously inside my shirt. The more tears I cried the more wet my shirt became. I desperately wanted to be the big girl my mom raised me to be. But I couldn't find the inner strength to face my fears in that moment. Something about death, my mom crying, and being in the hospital crippled me. I just wanted to rewind and pretend like the night never happened. That only happened in the movies.

She Kept Going Part 1 — Simmone Jones

That night my mom and I both cried ourselves to sleep praying silently for a miracle to bless us both. We were heading towards a storm that would change our family forever.

Chapter Four

August 1992

My legs were pumping hard, my tiny body glistening with sweat as I raced around the corner like a flash. I liked the feeling of the sun against my face and the wind at my back. It made me feel like I was flying, like I was the fastest thing on the ground, and nothing could stop me. I slowed down and took a breath. Georgia was always hot in the summertime, but I had heard from some people that winters could be a whole lot worse, in fact, winters up north has feet and feet of ice, cold, nasty snow. I wondered exactly how people could move around like that.

I hadn't known anything other than rural life, and my young mind couldn't picture anything other than fields, big blue skies and long, winding roads. I felt like I was big girl though. I stretched out my arms and sighed. My seventh birthday would be coming soon, and I didn't think I was a baby anymore. I heard a call from behind me and smiled.

Raymond was racing up to me, his face soaked in sweat and his small body heaving. "You left me!" he wailed, and I winked at him.

"You gotta be fast to catch me. You were beating' me all this time. Now you got me beating' you!" I remarked proudly.

Raymond rolled his eyes. "Whatever Jolene. You just got lucky. I don't even know why I agreed to race you. I always win."

"Well you didn't win this time," I told him and preened happily like a bird showing off its feathers. Raymond made a noise in his throat and nodded towards the street.

"You want to go again?" he asked, and I shrugged.

"I guess so. This time though, the loser is the one who doesn't make it past Mrs. Hawkins house first."

Raymond's eyes got real determined. I didn't feel fazed though. I knew I would win again I was getting faster and had been practicing a lot when Raymond wasn't around. Raymond was the same age as I was, but he was a little taller and had a head full of tightly coiled black hair. His dark toned complexion two shades deeper than mine—, nearly burnt sienna to my pecan skin tone. He lived across the street from me, my mother, my little sister and stepfather.

I don't know what it was that made us is friends with each other. I just remember looking at his bike and liked all the black and silver splashes on it. It looked cool and reminded me of the superheroes I sometimes saw on TV. He saw me looking and asked me if I wanted to race him. I told him "Yeah," and ever since, he and I had been pretty close.

I shook my head free of any thoughts and focused on the race. I had to win again. I grinned at Raymond and took off like a shot. I pushed myself hard and pedaled faster than I ever had before. I still only barely beat out Raymond, who had found some kind of newfound energy and was trying hard to catch up to me. I didn't care that he was only a few feet behind me. I had won again and that's what mattered.

I stuck out my tongue and teased him lightly. Raymond rolled his eyes again, but I could see he was smiling.

"I let you win that one," he told me. It was my turn to roll my eyes.

"No, you didn't," I told him, and we hopped off our bikes. We walked for a minute and we got closer to our houses. I could see that the care-free slumps of Raymond's shoulders were starting to disappear as we approached his house. His shoulders started to tense up and I wanted to ask him something, I just didn't know how to. I wondered if he was as sad, I could be sometimes.

I didn't always like how things were, and I suspected that he didn't like how things were at his house either. I didn't know too much about it though. His mother seemed nice enough and his dad—at least the man that was in the house, though gruff whenever I came around seemed okay.

I could hear his mother calling him from the steps. "Come on in boy," she was yelling. Raymond looked over at his stoop and shrugged. "Guess, I gotta see you later then," he told me. I nodded and gave him a little wave. He walked across the street, bike in tow. I watched until he reached his steps and I turned to my own house. I walked around the side and parked my bike. I wasn't too worried about anybody taking it. Everybody knew each other on the block and there wasn't much that went on most times. In other areas, it was a little different, but not here.

I walked inside and could hear the blare of the television. My mother was home from work, and I could see my stepfather on the couch. He was smoking weed and staring at the images on the screen. I could hear my mother in the kitchen, rummaging through the cabinets as the smell of food wafted to my nose. My little sister was in her playpen, babbling.

I walked into the kitchen and my mother frowned. "You sweaty," she told me. "I hope you don't plan on staying that way."

I shook my head and opened the fridge. It wasn't much inside, but I found some juice and decided to make do with that. I poured myself a glass and drank it down fast and hard. My mother was frying something, and she nodded over at the living room.

"I need you to help me with the baby," she told me. I nodded. I glanced over at her and noticed that she was moving slower than usual. Her belly was protruding, and she was rubbing her back and frowning a little. My other little sister was due in a few months.

"Okay, mama," I told her.

"Change her diaper for me," my mother commanded, and I put my glass in the sink and went into the living room where my sister's playpen was.

My sister was a year-old and going on two. I walked into the living room and she smiled at me. She started babbling something and I smiled back. I reached into the playpen and picked her up. She didn't fuss or anything. I think because she liked me a lot. I wondered if she understood I was her big sister.

She Kept Going Part 1   Simmone Jones

She liked it when I played with her and she followed me around the house when she could. I didn't know what it would be like when my other little sister got here, but I knew my mother would need my help. It made me feel a little grown-up to help change my sister's diapers and do things around the house sometimes.

I took my sister into the room we shared and laid her down on the bed. She was playing with her feet and I giggled and tickled her nose. She laughed and I began to change her diaper. I made quick work of it and threw the dirty diaper in the trash downstairs. I washed my hands and by the time I got back, my little sister had gotten off the bed and had decided to try to get something off the dresser.

"No!" I told her firmly and she and shot me a look of confusion.

"Let's go downstairs," I told her, and she toddled behind me. I stopped at the top of the stairs when I heard shouting. I pulled my sister behind me and waited to hear something further. My stepfather was yelling at my mother and she was screaming back.

I turned around and grabbed my little sister and began to walk back to the room. I hated when they fought like that. I wondered what it was about this time, but then I decided it didn't matter. I could hear more yelling and things being thrown. I huddled in the bed with my little sister and waited.

Sure enough, about an hour later, things died down. I breathed a sigh of relief. My mother called for me to come eat and grabbed my little sister and marched downstairs.

My mother made me a plate and I frowned. I didn't want what she cooked but I knew I had to eat it. My mother caught my frown and she gave me a stern look.

"You gon' eat everything on that plate too," she demanded, and I took my fork and began to eat. I looked over at her and noticed she had a dark mark on her face, like a bruise. I glanced over at my stepfather who had sat down at the table and had already begun eating.

I knew he had done it, but I also knew I couldn't say anything. I fixed my eyes on my plate and said nothing as he began to talk to my mother about his day. I knew he was in one of his moods, so I avoided eye contact with him.

My sister was in her highchair and I looked over at her and cooed a bit and encouraged her to eat. She glanced at me and gave me a toothy smile. She drooled a bit as she babbled and stuck a piece of food in her mouth.

My mother finally sat down after fixing her plate. I pushed my food around with my fork and glanced up at my stepfather; he caught my eye and sneered.

"What you looking' at me for?" he asked, and I quickly lowered my eyes and shrugged.

He cursed low and hard and I tried to keep my eyes on my plate. I had learned that it was easier to just avoid his attention when I could. My mother started talking to him, her tone soothing and placating and with a huff, he let go of his point and the conversation turned to something else.

I tuned them out and found myself lost in my own thoughts. I was excited to be going to the second grade. School was starting in a few weeks and that meant new clothes and school supplies. I munched on my food happily as I thought about all the things I'd learn and what kind of friends I'd make.

I finished my food before my mother did and I started clearing my plate. I was finally able to reach the sink, so I began running some water for the dishes. My stepfather was done eating as well, so I began to gather his dishes too. My mother started washing the dishes but said she had a headache and wanted to lay down. I helped her finish up what she could, and I headed to my room to play.

She Kept Going Part 1 — Simmone Jones

My sister was in her crib already and so I took out a book and began reading. It was just starting to get full dark outside even though the streetlights had been on for a while. I hated that too. The basic rule was to come in when the streetlights came on. Sometimes they came on when it wasn't even really dark outside. I pouted and flipped through my book some more. It didn't seem fair. My mother yelled for me to get out my "outside clothes" while I was sitting on the bed. I sighed and dragged myself to my dresser got out my pajamas and made my way to the bathroom. I ran my water and took a quick bath.

She Kept Going Part 1 — Simmone Jones

Afterwards, I went back to my room to read a bit before going to sleep. I found myself lost in the story about witches, princesses and fairies. After a long while, I could hear my sister's soft breathing from her crib as she fell into a deep sleep. After another long while, I was asleep too.

**

I awakened to the sound of food being prepared. I hopped out of bed and walked downstairs. My mother was frying up some food. My stomach growled and I sniffed happily. My mother smiled.

"I got some groceries. So, come eat," I grinned and nodded. I appreciated when my mother got good food. Things were often up and down, and I know my mother tried hard, so I tried really hard not to disappoint her. I sat down and looked over and saw my sister sitting in her highchair already.

My sister was babbling, and her face was already plastered with food. I made a mental note to clean her off after breakfast was over. I didn't hear my stepfather anywhere and I wondered if he was upstairs. I hoped not. I knew he was my sister's father and all, but I didn't always like him much. He seemed mostly distant to me and I felt like he was angry a lot. He had rare moments when he was funny and kind.

Sometimes, when he was in a really good mood, he bought me and my sister candy and flirted with my mother shamelessly as she giggled. I liked those kinds of days. But those kinds of days didn't come often enough, I thought.

"Where's Melvin?" I asked and glanced up at my mother who spooned me up a generous helping of bacon and eggs.

"He's already at work," she said, her lips tight.

I didn't say anything. I knew he didn't work. I knew whatever he did, my mother didn't like. They argued all the time about it though. She would tell him he needed to "get a real job." Sometimes she'd cry and tell him that he was going to get himself hurt or killed. I wondered what he was doing that would get him hurt like that. I tried asking my mother once, but she told me never to talk about things like that again.

I tried not to ask her anything that made her upset. I was always afraid she'd get mad at me, and I hated when that happened. I felt like it was just me and her against the world, and I didn't want her to ever feel like she couldn't count on me.

I sat down at the breakfast table and began to eat with gusto. I loved the taste of bacon on my tongue. I was chewing down when the phone rang, and my mother ran to get it. I tuned out my mother's conversation and concentrate on my food.

I knew from my mother's tone that it was a friend of my mom's. It was a lady named Lorraine that lived around the area. She and my mom hung out a lot. She was okay. She watched me and my sister sometimes when my mom had something to do or had to work.

My mother hung up the phone. "Lorraine is coming by baby," she told me. I nodded in between bites.

My mother was already cleaning up her plate. "I gotta get to this shift. They don't care that I'm pregnant though. Oh no, they just have to have me come in and fill in," my mother complained.

I was glad that Lorraine was coming by and not Melvin. I didn't really like it when he babysat me. Lorraine let me watch what little television we had. We didn't have many channels, but she didn't hog the TV like Melvin did when he came by. Lorraine would often just sit and read magazines. She was good for helping me with my homework and puzzles and stuff.

I quickly ate breakfast and soon Lorraine was walking in the door right as my mother was waddling out of it. They greeted each other and my mother waved goodbye.

Lorraine gave me a smile as she walked in and put her purse down. She cooed at my sister and touched her cheek.

"Hey babies," she said, and I waved at her.

"Hi Lorraine."

Lorraine hummed in answer and plopped down on the couch. "Did you brush your teeth and wash up?" she asked as she eyed my pajamas.

I shook my head. She sucked her teeth. "Now you know that's just nasty. Go wash up and brush your teeth. Change your clothes and get ready for the day."

"Yes ma'am," I mumbled. I then remembered why I didn't like Lorraine sometimes. She could be stern.

I made my way up to the bathroom and did as she asked. When I was done, I padded down the stairs and hopped next to her on the couch.

Chapter Five

"Can I go outside?" I asked her. She looked hesitant.

"Pleaaaase?" I begged.

"Okay. But stay where I can see you. Don't be all out in the neighborhood either."

"Okay!"

I grabbed a jump rope and ran out the door before she could change her mind.

There were already a group of girls out playing double Dutch. Two of them I knew from school and the rest were girls from the area.

"Can I play?" I asked the one girl, a tall, darker skinned girl with lots of hair and dimples. She was the leader of the group and she looked down at me and made a face.

"You can have a turn after her," she pointed at a girl wearing all pink with short pigtails in her hair. "But you gotta turn first. You aren't double-handed, are you?"

I shook my head. "I turn good," I assured her.

She handed me the rope and I began to turn. I chimed in as the girls chanted and sang. One of the girls stood near me, waiting for the right moment to jump in. I studied her jumping style for a minute and got lost in the song and looked over the rope as it sailed through the air.

I could see a bunch of police cars at the end of the block. It wasn't anything I hadn't seen before, but there was something familiar about some of the people down there. I was trying to turn and look at the same time.

She Kept Going Part 1   Simmone Jones

There were a bunch of guys standing around. Some of them were being handcuffed. I glanced again and narrowed my eyes. There was something about one of them that just looked—familiar.

I glanced some more and then my mouth dropped. The man they were putting into the police car was my stepfather Melvin.

My mother was crying on the couch and my sister was sitting in her lap babbling wildly. Lorraine was rubbing my mother's back and saying something in a low voice. I didn't know what to do, so I sat in the corner with my coloring book, trying to block out what was happening. Was this because of Melvin? Was Melvin in jail? Did he do something bad? I suspected it had something to do with the guys on the corner. My mother warned me to stay away from them.

She told me that they did bad things, especially to little girls like me.

My mother's sobs became whimpers and I looked back a few times to see Lorraine blotting my mother's face with a tissue.

"He ain't no good girl. I don't even know why you even bother with him," Lorraine said, her face was pulled into a disappointing frown.

"He my baby's father," my mother replied, and Lorraine shrugged.

"That ain't got nothing to do with a hill of beans. That man is gon' drive you crazy. He ain't got no job Trice…,"

My mother sucked her teeth. "I'm tired of his dealing'. All the time. Dealing them damn drugs. Got him a job at that store, but he don't want that. He rather have me up here crying' and hollering--," my mother cried a bit more and Lorraine made soothing noises, kind of like how she does with my sister when she's upset.

My sister was confused, and she was standing up on shaky legs patting my mother's face with chubby little hands. I felt powerless. I didn't know what to do to make things right. I hesitated a moment and rocked back and forth on the balls of my feet. I watched my mother for a moment more and then walked over to the couch. I sat down beside her.

I patted her arm. "Mama, don't cry. If we need money, I can get a job," I told her.

My mother was crying, but her tears turned to laughter. "This child," she said and shook her head. She wiped away her tears. "You so funny!"

She laughed some more and then gave me a big hug. "You sho'll try' best to take care of yo' momma don't ya?"

I nodded and she planted a kiss on my forehead. "You ain't got to worry about that baby. Not for a long time. I want you to stay in those books and be a kid."

I nodded, but a part of me felt as if I needed to do more than just be a kid. I didn't like seeing my mother cry.

"Jolene, take your sister upstairs and play for a while. Me and yo' momma talking' grown folks' business."

I nodded and reluctantly got off the couch. I waggled my finger in front of my sister and she slid from beside my mother and toddled over to me. I walked her up the stairs and we went to my room.

I listened to the sound of my mother and Lorraine's voices as they wafted up the stairs. Our walls were pretty thin, but I couldn't make out what they were saying. Every now and again, I'd hear a word or two, but it wasn't much.

I pulled my sister to me and then picked her up. I placed her in her crib and she immediately went for one of the toys she had there. While she babbled and played, I sat on my bed, looking up at the ceiling. I wondered briefly if there was anything, I could do to help my mother. I wondered if I could help at Mr. Diego's store. He seemed real nice. I could clean up or something. Then I remembered how my mother didn't want me doing those things. She wanted me to stay a kid.

I sighed in frustration and grabbed my book from the nightstand. I loved to read. Sometimes reading was the only way I could calm down. Whenever I felt bad about something, I enjoyed dreaming about princesses, dragons and magic beans.

I sometimes liked the fantasy world more than the real one. I didn't like all the shouting and screaming in my house. I hated how Melvin talked down to my mother, called her names and things like that. I told myself that I would never let anyone talk to me that way. I thought my mother was so pretty; she could get anyone she wanted. I just didn't understand why she wanted Melvin. He wasn't very nice.

I grabbed my ball and began bouncing it against the wall. My sister looked on in fascination. I smiled at her and got up and handed her the ball.

"You want to play?" I asked her. She tried to grab the ball with her chubby little hands, but it fell into her crib. I giggled and handed it to her.

"'Lene," she said and looked up at me, her eyes big and innocent.

I grinned. She just called my name. Well part of it anyway. I felt my heart melt. I loved my little sister. I wanted to protect her from everything I could. I was her big sister after all.

I heard footsteps and I turned to look at the doorway. Lorraine was there, giving me a calm smile.

"Your momma need some time alone so I'm gon' take the baby. You go play outside."

I nodded and watched as Lorraine cross the space between us and grabbed the baby. The baby adored Lorraine and cooed wildly. Lorraine tickled her under her chin and cooed back, getting a big smile filled with sparse teeth and gums from the baby.

Chapter Six

I grabbed a few toys and bounced happily down the stairs. I didn't see my mother and wondered where she went. Lorraine followed me down the stairs and she tapped me affectionately on the head.

"Don't be going' all through the neighborhood either. Stay where we can see you."

I pouted. "But I want to ride my bike and go to the park. Please? It's not far away."

I could see Lorraine considering the option. She looked back behind her and then back to me.

"Okay. But don't tell your momma. Don't be going far either."

I grinned and shot outside. I grabbed my bike and raced over to my friend's house. I knocked on his door and heard shuffling. His mother came to the door a cigarette in hand.

I cleared my throat. "Can Raymond come out and play?"

His mother gave me a look I could decipher and then she looked behind her. "Yeah. Ray!" she called out.

I could hear Raymond answering back and then quick footsteps. Raymond saw me and sprinted to the door.

"Let's ride bikes!" I told him excitedly. He grinned and nodded. He burst out of the door past his mom and we headed down the stairs. I parked my bike right next to his, around the side. He unhooked his bike from the lock and we began walking our bikes to the front.

"Let's head to the park, "he suggested.

I looked around. I could still see my house, but I didn't want to stay in the area. Not with the man around.

"Okay," I decided and we began rushing down the street at high speed. We biked down the avenue, with the wind whipping our faces and I could hear a laugh escape my throat as I began to outpace Raymond. He shot me a look and I stuck out my tongue at him, feeling slightly triumphant.

"Whatever," he said with a nonchalant shrug. I laughed good and hard and we continued biking towards the park.

After two hours in the park Raymond and I decided it was time to head on home. We were a few feet away from his house when we both overheard people yelling. We both looked at each other with curiosity and concern in our eyes.

I didn't know what to say or do so I kept quiet.

"I gotta go," Raymond told me and I nodded.

I could hear his mother fussing but tuned it out as I biked home.

I pulled my bike over to the side of my house and then traipsed to the front steps. I jogged up and went inside. Lorraine was sitting in the living room with the baby and I could see my mother in the kitchen talking to someone. The other person had their back to me, so I couldn't see.

I walked in further and a big smile came across my face when I recognized who it was.

It was my Granddad George Dupree. He was my mother's stepdad and one of my favorite people in the whole world. He always had candy to give me, and he took me and my sister to church a lot. We haven't been going a lot, mostly because momma been having

Melvin over a lot and I knew Granddad Dupree didn't like him much.

"Hey Granddad Dupree!" I grinned and he opened his arms to me, an invitation for a big hug.

"Hey there, big girl! How you doing?"

"I'm alright," I told him as he embraced me hard. I relished his attentions and face smiled.

"I was just telling' yo' momma I'm coming' to get you two tomorrow. You ain't been in church in forever. And see kids need guidance. This is the age to get 'em Trice."

My mother mumbled some agreement and rested her back in the chair. I could tell she was wanting to smoke, but since she had gotten pregnant, she had given up on that. She was rubbing her belly in big, wide circles instead. I wondered what the baby was doing inside her.

"I know, I know," my mother stated. Granddad Dupree nodded and then looked over at me. "See, her and her sister, get the word of God in them ain't nothing' that can get them to do wrong."

My mother tensed. I could sense the conversation was about to veer into an area my mother didn't like because she was scratching her hair and frowning.

"See, I know you love hard, Trice. But sometimes, we got to let love go that ain't good. All love ain't good love. Know what I'm saying'?"

My mother said nothing for a moment and then whispered. "You right."

"They need a man to teach them what they supposed to be doing'. You think that boy is doing' that? You think he got his head on, right? And where is he now? "Granddad Dupree questioned.

My mother looked away, and I could see a fleeting look of shame cover her soft womanly features. "You know where he is."

"You do too. And you still wit him," Granddad Dupree shook his head. "Makes no damn sense. You young girls. I tell ya. I'm going to pick these little ones up tomorrow morning. You gon' be home?"

"Yeah. We are home."

Granddad Dupree nodded his head and their conversation turned to other things. I bounced in place for a second on his lap and then slid off. I happily marched into the living room just in time to see Lorraine feeding my sister a cookie.

"Oooh," I pointed. "I want one too!"

Lorraine laughed and reached into her purse. She got another cookie and handed it to me. "Thank you, ma'am," I told her. My sister looked at her cookie then at Lorraine. She tried to babble thank you too and Lorraine laughed.

"She sho'll is funny," Lorraine said, and I bit into the cookie. It was chocolate chip.

I gobbled it down and played with my sister for a bit.

She Kept Going Part 1 — Simmone Jones

I was glad I was going to church with Granddad Dupree. It was always fun.

****

The next morning, I awakened bright and early. I didn't need any prodding. I was happy to shuffle myself into the bathroom and take a bath. I got cleaned up in record time and brushed my teeth. I did my hair and then came back to my room. My little sister was just waking up. She clambered up to standing position with a grin and gave me a drool smile.

"Hey!" I told her. I walked over and gave her a big kiss on the nose. She laughed and I tickled her a bit before going into my closet to find something to wear.

I grabbed a pretty, frilly dress that my mother had bought me a month before. She had splurged a bit on clothes during that time and for some reason it had made Melvin mad. I don't know what he said to her, I just remember them fighting and then him smoking afterwards. I shook my head free of those negative thoughts. I was going to church with Granddad Dupree. That was all that mattered.

I put on my dress and was slipping on a pair of socks when my mother poked her head in and gave me a smile. "You dressed already huh?"

I nodded and she walked into the room to grab the baby. "I'm gon' get her dressed too."

An hour later, both my sister and I were all set and ready for Granddad Dupree to come and get us.

We heard a honk and my mother peeked outside. "Alright y'all."

My mother walked us outside and got my sister strapped into the car seat that Granddad Dupree had in his car. I slid in next to her and we were soon off and motoring down the street. I looked back to see my mother waving at us before she slipped back inside.

We arrived at the church not long after. It was small and I could tell that it was going to be another Sunday where only ten people or so showed up. Most of the folk went to the big mega church not far away, but Granddad Dupree didn't seem too concerned about that. He told us that mega churches loved pizzazz and the lights and all that, but they didn't really preach the word of God.

Granddad Dupree was a deacon at the church. He'd sit in the corner of the room near the pastor and shout amen frequently. Every now and again he'd toss a stern look in my direction to tell me to sit still and be quiet. Granddad Dupree always warned me of a popping on the butt. But he never could put his hands on me. If I caused any trouble, he'd tell my momma and have her whoop my behind good.

I liked the time we spent at the church because while Granddad Dupree assisted the pastor occasionally. I helped tidy up the church in the back and ate food that one of the ladies cooked.

My sister was always on someone's lap and I got to eat a meal in peace. I enjoyed that time. As much as I loved my sister and mother, there was no Melvin, no having to help and just me, some food and sweet old ladies that gave me some time to myself.

After I ate, I usually played on the back of the stairs or I would go up in the balcony and listen to the choir sing a tune. I sometimes wondered if it bothered my granddad that not that many people came to the church. I knew if I was a pastor and no one came to my church, I'd be sad. Granddad Dupree didn't seem to mind. He told me it's not about quantity, but quality. He said he would rather lead a flock of the faithful than a herd of evildoers.

I wondered what that meant. Sometimes I think that Granddad Dupree just liked what he did on Sundays. Maybe that's what we're supposed to do as adults. We get to grow up and do the stuff that we liked. Sometimes Granddad Dupree would ask me what I liked to do. I wasn't sure what I liked to do. Maybe not yet. I liked to play, and I liked to draw. I really, really liked reading. Maybe if there was a job for someone that liked to draw and read, I could do that.

She Kept Going Part 1 — Simmone Jones

The church service was wrapping up and I looked down on the sparse congregation. There was one old lady, Mrs. Simmons who was all the way in the back. I think she was sleeping. Old people did that a lot. Once the pastor told everyone to have a blessed day, I ran downstairs to the basement happily. I knew what was coming next: a big, wonderful lunch.

Down in the church basement we all gathered to eat a delicious spread. My eyes jumped outside of my head in excitement. I knew my stomach would be filled with so much joy from eating all of the delicious food. The air was filled with different aromas that made your spirit want to jump for joy inside your body. While my little sister was being passed around and smothered in church lady kisses. I began to jump inside the small line of hungry patrons ready to eat. There were barbeque meatballs, potato salad, cornbread muffins, fried chicken, green beans, and fruit bowl for dessert. I knew my mother would have loved to be here to get a good plate. It would have given her sometime to not be on her feet all night making dinner. The church mothers smiled down at me as I pointed gleefully at the options in front of me. I nodded my head and flashed a toothy grin as they asked, "You want some food baby." Today was one of those rare days where I didn't mind being called baby. I was one happy and stuffed kid.

Granddad Dupree sat at the head of the table. His heavy beard, soft teddy bear eyes, and oily black leather skin complimented him well. People at the church often looked at him for guidance. People of all ages were pulled into his loving charm and felt his warmth as soon as you entered the room. I'd found a seat right next to Granddad Dupree as food particles landed inside his beard as he smacked his lips. He smiled at me with love in his eyes. He whispered over at me, "Did you enjoy yourself today little princess?"

I nodded proudly like a big girl. I stared Granddad Dupree back inside his dark brown eyes and exuded the love he'd given me so freely over the years.

"Well, that's good baby girl. You know you are always welcome in the house of the Lord. Always." He grinned.

"Always?" I questioned.

Granddad Dupree released a hearty laugh that caused his beard to tremor slightly.

"Always." He repeated.

His words stuck to my soul like water on a hot summer day. In that moment, I believed that as long as Granddad Dupree was alive, I'd always have a safe space in the world. That place would always begin and end with his heart and mine.

Chapter Seven

Raymond and I were sitting on the porch eating ice cream sandwiches. My mother had thrown some in the shopping cart as a special treat for my good behavior. Raymond nearly ate the wrapping paper he was so excited.

"Dang, ain't you ever had ice cream before." I joked.

Raymond shrugged and ignored me. He knew if he didn't eat the ice cream fast enough the flies and the ants would take it.

The screen door was unlocked as my mother allowed a stiff cool breeze to enter the front door. The screen door was to protect against the bugs and insects from coming inside the house. Every now and then a fly or two would sneak inside the house and drive my mother crazy. I knew it was mostly my fault the flies got inside. My mother would start ranting and raving until the cows came home. I believed the bugs got on her nerves more than I did.

On this particular day, it was hotter than normal. Usually it would be so hot in the country Raymond and I could find a shaded tree to catch a cool breeze. Today, it was so hot outside that not even the wind rustled through the trees. The sun swallowed Raymond and I both whole and held us captive in the daylight. I could feel the burning rays on my skin. I didn't mind that much. It was better for me to be outside with nature than stuck in the house staring at the ceiling. I thank Raymond felt the same way. He never liked going home much. Whenever it was time for him to go back, I felt like a part of him died slowly in the darkness of night.

For me, things were finally making sense again. My mother hours had eased up at the store. We'd reconnect over the past few days since Grandpa Dupree took me to church. Maybe some of the things he shared touched my heart more than I realized. I just decided to share what I learned with my mother. I could see pain in her eyes. I hugged her tightly around her neck and told her everything was going to be alright. I don't know if she believed me. But the way her arms wrapped around my tiny frame I knew she felt something on the inside. A part of me felt relieved and happy to have my mother back to myself. Our lives were much better without Melvin in the picture. I never realized how much he affected our lives on a daily basis. I wondered silently in my mind could our happiness last forever. Or would the devil show up and steal our joy again any day now?

Raymond and I were coming back from the park on our bikes. The day had past us by and our stomachs were growling. We joked about how hungry we were and what we could eat.

"Man, I'm so hungry I could eat a horse." Raymond joked.

I laughed and smiled back at my friend.

"I'm so hungry I could eat a gorilla and two giraffes."

"You're so greedy Jolene. You want all the animals to yourself."

I shook my head. "I'll give you my leftovers, maybe."

She Kept Going Part 1

Simmone Jones

We were pulling up towards my house when I saw a red Cadillac in the yard. I didn't recognize the car, so my heart began to race. Raymond and I both slowed down and looked at each other with confusion in our eyes. With my mouth agape, I watched from a distance as a hand hang out the passenger window. A lit cigarette on the far end of a dark skin man hand. Music came blaring from the car. It sounded like rap. I couldn't make out the artist or the song. I was too caught up in the idea of the mystery man in the yard.

"Jolene is that…." Raymond inquired softly.

"I don't know." I replied.

"It looks like him. But whose car is that? I've never seen it before?" Raymond questioned.

Raymond's mouth was saying all the things floating around inside my head. I couldn't believe my eyes. Melvin was back and he'd brought trouble with him. I didn't like the idea of my mother and sister being in the house alone with him. My blood began to boil as the heat caused my eyes to sweat.

"Jolene, don't do anything stupid." Raymond warned. He placed his arm across my bike.

"I'm not. I just need to make sure that my mom and sister are okay."

"Good. I'll come with you." Raymond suggested.

"No. You go on home. I'll be alright."

Raymond looked at me as if he'd seen a ghost. I knew he didn't believe the words coming out of my mouth. At the moment, I didn't need him too. I just needed to get to my family.

**

I parked my bike on the side of the house. I walked right past the red Cadillac like it wasn't even there. I knew Melvin was my sister's father. He didn't mean anything to me. I only tolerated him for the sake of my mother. Even at seven years old I knew he was a bad seed and wanted nothing to do with him.

I stepped onto the porch. Before I could open the screen door, Melvin called for me. I cringe and shut my eyes. My heart starts beating faster than before. I slowly turn around to face Melvin. He's leaning outside of the car with a dingy wife beater shirt on. He flashes a toothy grin in my direction and instructs me to come to him. I do so begrudgingly. I take slow deliberate steps with my eyes planted on the ground. With balled fist I step two feet in front of Melvin. He opens the car door and jumps out. Within seconds he picks me up off the ground and twirls me in the air. He hugs me tightly as the stench of beer and cigarettes permeates through his skin. His skin is dank from sweating in the hot Georgia sun all day.

I release a mild mannered hey into the air. My eyes flash towards his hefty sized friend seating in the car eating chicken wings. He doesn't wave hello or say anything. He just continues eating and glances at me occasionally. He looks like a bad man.

"Jolene, you sho have gotten big since the last time I saw you." Melvin suggest as he plants me back on the ground in front of him.

"Okay." I state unsure on how to answer his statement.

Melvin and his chapped lips smile back at me. He squats down and whispers to me.

"Things gone be different this time. I'm not going away anymore, ya hear." Melvin suggests.

"I know." I retort.

"Good, now me and your momma have some business to take care of later. You want to be a big girl and watch your baby sis for me."

I nod my head quickly.

"Good. You go on in the house and get washed up for dinner. I'll be in a few." Melvin replies.

I do as I'm told. As soon as I open the front door my mother is standing there rubbing her protruding belly. She's dressed in a tee shirt and oversized shorts. She looks like she's just woken up from a nap and not in the mood for Melvin's stuff. I greet her and tell her I'm going to the bathroom to wash up for dinner.

My mother doesn't utter a word. Instead she looks right past me and at Melvin and his friend sitting in the car. My stomach began to twist into tight knots. I could tell by the way my mother received Melvin that a mighty storm was brewing on the inside of her soul. I knew that today would be one I would never forget.

She Kept Going Part 1 — Simmone Jones

We were having catfish and French fries for dinner when Melvin stumbled inside the house drunk as a skunk. My mother refused to allow him inside the house with the cigarettes, drinking, and loud music. She said he would scare the girls and when he was ready, he could sleep it off on the couch. I was proud of my mother. She was finally standing her ground when it came to Melvin. I knew it wasn't easy for her loving a man that didn't love you the way you deserved. Lorraine always told my mother that life was all about choices. I guess she finally listened for once. This time she was choosing herself and us.

"Got damn it stank up in here!" Melvin exclaimed. He slurred his words and wobbled inside the front door. I looked at him with shame inside my eyes. His imposter I'd met in the driveway was gone. He was back to his old self. This was the Melvin I knew all too well.

Melvin slammed the front door behind him and flopped down on the couch. His presence shifted the peaceful and tranquil dinner we were having into chaos and confusion. My little sister began to coo inside her seat as she meshed French fries and ketchup across her face. Her babbling continued to grow inside my ear. I watched as my mother began to battle within her inner self. She clutched her sounds frequently and glanced back at Melvin on the couch. Her once sunny and positive demeanor was slowly disappearing behind the wrinkles in her forehead and slumped shoulders. My eyes bulged at the sight of worry on my mother's face. I wanted to protect her and my sisters. I just didn't know how at the moment. I slowly ate the cold French fries inside my plate as Melvin grumbled underneath his breath.

"I need a damn beer...that will knock my ass out something good tonight." Melvin voiced.

"You've had enough Melvin. I'll help you get comfortable soon." My mother responded timidly.

She avoided eye contact and stared down at the obedient food on her plate. Her right hand began trembling as she tried to nourish her body and keep the tears from falling from her eyes. The longer I sat there the more I became concerned about my mother, sister, and I. We were in danger and no one was coming to save us.

"Shut up woman!" Melvin exclaimed.

"That's enough Melvin. Respect my house or get out and I mean it this time." My mother replied.

She straightened her back and spoke evenly in Melvin's direction. I could feel things beginning to get worse before they got better. My little sister had meshed enough fries on her face and the ketchup stained her fluffy cheeks. Her eyes were growing heavy by the second. I knew within a matter of minutes she would become agitated and sleepy.

She Kept Going Part 1 — Simmone Jones

"Momma, can we be excused?" I asked politely.

My mother looked at me with tears in her eyes. I knew she was regretful for allowing Melvin back into our lives. She was guilty of trying to love the good in a man that meant her all bad. My mother was human and flawed. My mother bit down on her bottom lip and nodded her head. I picked up my little sister and carried her upstairs. I cleaned her face with a warm washcloth and changed her diaper. She pulled my hair gently and smiled back at me grateful. I placed her inside my arms on my tiny bed and held her close to me.

We were lying in bed when I heard my mother wailing out loud. From the sounds of her cries she was in more pain than before. She wailed so loudly that I could feel a tear fall from my eyes. I tried to shield my little sister from the sound of the wailing, but it was too late. She cried in my arms that night for hours. We could hear the sound of glass shattering and hitting the floor. Curiosity got the best of me and I sneaked my head down the stairs. I didn't want my mother to leave this world without someone coming to her rescue. Melvin didn't see me or maybe he wasn't paying close attention. I watched him ball his fist and punch my mother repeatedly. My mother did her best to protect herself and baby. But Melvin had blacked out and not become himself anymore. It was as if something had taken over him.

I couldn't believe my eyes. I began to scream stop loud as I could. I screamed so loudly that my throat began to burn. Melvin looked up at me with his fist in the air. He looked at me with bloodshot eyes like a ghost had suddenly appeared before him.

Melvin blinked in my direction for a few seconds and slowly lowered his hand. My mother removed her hand from her face and stared back at me. Her face bruised and wet. Melvin stood on his two feet and wiped his forehead. His shirt ripped and bloodied. He took a few deep breaths and began to walk out the front door. As soon as the front door was closed, I ran to my mother's side. I called Lorraine and told her to come quick. My mother rested on the floor afraid and abused to the point where she couldn't care for herself. I held her hand and kissed her cheek. I didn't know what else to do. I just knew that I needed her as much as she needed me. Together we could get through anything. This was the promise I made to myself and my mother for the rest of my life.

Chapter Eight

We were sitting in the break room when the doctors pulled my momma and Lorraine to the side. Lorraine held my mommas' hand and guided her slowly towards the doctor. We'd been in the hospital for weeks waiting on Melvin to fully recover from his injuries. Some days were better than others. The doctors warned my mother that they didn't

She Kept Going Part 1   Simmone Jones

know if Melvin would make it out of the woods. The bullet had pierced a nerve in his chest which caused his lungs to clasp frequently. Melvin wasn't my favorite person in the world. I didn't want to see him die. I'd never seen my mother pray on her knees so much. She'd hold my hand tightly outside Melvin's hospital and talk to God in a whisper. I'd never talked to God before in this way. It was new and different for me. My momma told me God was always listening we just needed to open up and talk to Him. He would make everything alright.

I wanted to believe every word coming out of my momma's mouth. I could tell by the look in her eyes that she believed in God more than the doctors. Despite everything Melvin had put her through she still loved him deeply. I watched from a distance as the doctors nodded their heads confidently as they spoke to my momma. I could hear a sigh of relief coming out of her mouth.

"Praise God!" She exclaimed. "Thank you, doctor!"

Lorraine hugged my momma tightly and urged me to come over and join the hug. I carried my baby sister on my hip and hugged my momma around her waist.

"What did the doctors say?" I asked curiously.

"They said Melvin is in stable condition and is ready to come home. Isn't that good news baby girl?"

For the first time in weeks, my momma smiled down at me. I didn't have the courage to tell her that I didn't want Melvin back with us. I just wanted us to be a family without him. I knew that would break her heart and she'd suffered enough. I did what any good daughter would do. I lied.

Chapter Nine

September 2000

Raina wanted chicken noodles for dinner and my baby sister, Kima wanted anything she could get her hands on. I only knew how to boil water in the microwave. If it wasn't microwaveable, I wasn't allowed to cook it. I studied my algebra homework and tried

She Kept Going Part 1   Simmone Jones

my best to keep my eyes on my six-year-old sister. Raina and I were only four years apart. But she depended on me to do everything for her like I was her parent. She was bossy and spoiled at times. Kima was still innocent most days. That is if you didn't interrupt her during her favorite TV shows or eat up her favorite snacks.

I'd grown up and filled out as my Grandma Cookie would say to me over the phone from Mississippi. I had curves and hair in places I couldn't explain. I'd traded in my tomboy days with Raymond to dancing in my bedroom mirror and playing in makeup.

She Kept Going Part 1   Simmone Jones

On some days I felt like a young woman with a bright future ahead of myself. Other days, I felt like giving up on everything and everyone. I wish I felt as grown up on the inside the way my body did on the outside. I'd be lying if I said things got better after Melvin was shot in the front yard a few years ago. Not quite so much in my opinion. Things continued to go from bad to worst.

When Melvin came home from the hospital momma waited on him hand and foot. She catered to his every need to make sure that he was comfortable inside their bedroom. He laid up in the bed for six weeks moaning and complaining most days. He was louder than the television in the living room. I tried to ignore him as much as possible. For the longest time, I was afraid to go near Melvin after seeing him in the hospital. I'd never seen someone with so many tubes and machines on their body. For the longest time the hospital gave me nightmares. I remember trying to go back to school a week after Melvin entered the hospital. All I could do was cry and think about how badly my momma was hurting on the inside. My momma ended up pulling me out of school for a few days. I was grateful. I just wanted to be around my family.

I knew things were going to be different when Melvin came home. I just didn't know exactly how different. I noticed my momma smiling more everyday she got a chance to wake up next to Melvin. I often wondered if that was what true love looked like as an adult. You love someone despite their faults. *Were you supposed to forgive them for all the pain they caused you? Was it really that easy to love someone unconditionally? Did love really conquer all, even the ugly parts of a person?*

I knew my questions needed answers. I just didn't believe that my momma was the right one to answer them for me. So, I kept my mouth quiet most days in the house. I didn't want to upset Melvin. Since that eventful night momma told me to always try to be on my best behavior and to respect Melvin. Now I didn't really know what she meant at the time. I figured Melvin owed us everything and more for putting up with his foolishness and shenanigans. But my momma didn't see things the way I did. I was just a naïve girl in her eyes. I had a lot more to learn about the world. In some ways, I figured my momma did too.

Once Melvin was fully recovered that's when things got really crazy in our lives. Momma had lost at least two or three jobs. Seemed to me like she was trying to keep an eye on Melvin more than she was her three kids. Even though I was fourteen I knew very little about raising a family. My momma would tell me to make noodles for dinner or a bowl of cereal before bed. She'd walk out the door with her purse on her shoulder and eyes red. It would be the pit of night and she'd be gone until the morning and return around afternoon. She would be

She Kept Going Part 1 — Simmone Jones

looking for Melvin. I knew at fourteen that Melvin was no good for my momma and us. He was like a rotten apple on the inside. He looked good on the outside until you got up real close and personal. I knew better to question my momma or her choices, so I did as I was told most days. I'd get up early to wash my sister's faces, make breakfast, and drop them off at school/daycare. Running all over town early in the morning usually caused me to be late school. I'd pray none of my teacher would notice. Some of them didn't care enough to ask me what was going on at home. The others just shook their heads in my direction and made notes in my record. I was late for school one particular morning when my math teacher Mr. Hightower pulled me into the hallway.

"Jolene, you've been late to class every day this week. Is everything okay at home?"

I nodded my head and averted my eyes to my untied shoelaces. I fidgeted with my hands for a bit and stood nervously in the hallway.

"Are you telling me the truth?" Mr. Hightower questioned.

"Yes sir."

Mr. Hightower cleared his throat and folded his arms. He took two steps towards me and whispered, "Do you need to tell me something in private?"

I knew exactly what he meant by private. I knew better than to tell him about my personal business at home. My momma always told me to keep the government and white folks out of our business. I figured that meant teachers and principals too.

"No, I'm fine." I lied.

Mr. Hightower sighed and took a step back. "Jolene your grades are dropping rapidly, and I'm concerned. I'm going to schedule a meeting with your parents. After class give me your mom's work and cell number."

"Yes Mr. Hightower."

My heart began to sink inside my stomach. I knew Mr. Hightower was only looking out for my best interest. He was a good teacher overall. But I knew if he found out my mom was leaving me alone at home at night or that Melvin sold drugs out the house we would be in big trouble.

Chapter Ten

One night while I was standing in the kitchen washing dishes and the telephone rang. My momma was at work. She'd picked up a night shift job at the local nursing home as an aide. She'd make dinner in the afternoon and leave it wrapped up in foil on the stove. She'd give me specific instructions on how to warm up the food for dinner. I followed her instructions daily with little to no help from Melvin at all. In my eyes, Melvin had become a glorified babysitter that kept my mommas' bed warm at night. I was halfway through washing the dishes when the phone rang. I looked at the clock on the wall and it was a quarter past seven. I'd told my best friend Nicole that I would tell her everything Deonte Johnson told me about his date with Michelle Robinson last weekend. Nicole wanted to date Deonte from the moment she laid eyes on him in health class. She was too shy to speak up for herself at times. I was cool with Deonte because we grew up in the same neighborhood. I didn't find him that cute in my eyes. Every time he'd open his mouth, he'd give me an unnecessary shower.

I told Nicole I'd be done with my chores by eight and I would be free to talk on the phone. I didn't tell her about Melvin and his mood swings. Some days he was cool as a summer breeze. Other days he was as hot as fish grease. There were very little times where he was in the middle with his mood. I was hardly on his good side this one particular night. He'd gotten on my case about getting in the house late. I'd stop by the corner store on my way home from school. I knew Melvin was waiting on me to get home and turn into a maid, so I took my time getting home. As soon as I walked through the front door, he had something smart to say to me.

"I guess you think you grown now don't you." He stated sternly.

I rolled my eyes and walked past him into the living room.

"Whatever." I whispered.

Melvin slammed the front door shut and walked up behind me. He grabs my right around tightly and turns my body towards him.

"What did you just say?!" He yells.

I began to wince and beg for him to let go of my arm.

"Let me go Melvin, you're hurting me." I plead.

Melvin raises his baritone voice and leans in closer towards me. I can tell by his red bulging eyes that he's been up all night.

"Watch your mouth little girl or I will show you who's grown around here. You understand?"

I nod my head and Melvin releases my arm. Once he was out of ear shot, I cursed him out something good inside my head. He wasn't my daddy and I felt very strongly about him putting his dirty hands on me. After fifteen minutes inside my bedroom I began to take care of my chores and responsibilities.

I tried my best to stay out of Melvin's way after the incident earlier. But I could tell by his lack of communication and mean mug on his face that he had one more bone to pick with me. Something told me that I was going to be taking a risk answering the ringing phone. But I knew Nicole wasn't going to stop calling until I answered the phone. Whatever Melvin had in store for me I was willing to accept it. I dried the soap studs off my hands and reached for the receiver on the phone. Before I could even say hello, Nicole was going a mile a minute.

"Don't even lie and tell me you didn't see Deonte today at school. I know y'all in the same homeroom together." Nicole stated eagerly.

I laughed, "Yeah, we are. He asked me about you if you want to know…."

Nicole screamed. "Tell me every word friend!"

Dial tone.

Melvin pressed the button the phone to end the call. He stood over me anger brewing in his eyes.

"No phone calls tonight."

I rolled my eyes and said, "My momma knows I be talking to Nicole before I go to bed."

Melvin shook his head and said, "Your momma's not here. I am. My rules."

I took a deep breath and rolled my eyes once more. "I hate being here with you." I whispered underneath my breath.

I began to walk away from the phone on the wall and upstairs to my room. The dishes were done, and I figured I'd had enough of Melvin battles for one day. I was halfway out of the kitchen when I felt a strike against my back.

I cried out loudly as the large leather belt whipped across my back. It hurt so bad that it felt like my soul jumped out of my body. I turned around quickly to see Melvin wrapping the belt around his right hand again. A crooked smile began to cover his face as he raised his hand and began to spank me with the belt. I tried to run and hide behind the furniture inside the apartment. But the little furniture we had wasn't good enough to save me. I cried so loudly that I knew my little sisters cried for me. I could hear their screams on top of my own. Melvin didn't care if his belt was causing bruises to my light brown skin. He was on a power trip and I fell right into his lap. He beat me so bad that I bit down on my tongue and tasted my own blood.

By the time it was over I could hardy move from the fetal position on the floor. I was in too much pain. Melvin didn't care about me.

He just turned the television up louder to tune out my moans. I laid on the floor until the next morning when my mother returned home. She didn't say anything. She just put coco butter on my skin and told me to get ready for school.

Chapter Eleven

I could hold a grudge longer than anyone in my family. Once you hurt me, I was going to get revenge on you. Melvin was on my bad side. There was nothing no one on earth who could convince me otherwise. Everything about Melvin made my skin crawl. The only person I could confide in was my best friend Nicole. She lived alone with her mom in a two-bedroom apartment. Her mom worked all the time and normally left her home alone. Some days I wanted to trade lives with Nicole. Every time I'd come to school in a turtleneck and extra jacket. Nicole knew I'd gotten spanked by Melvin and she'd escort me into the girl's bathroom to look at my bruises.

"That motherfucker!" Nicole exclaimed.

"Is it that bad?"

"It's worse than I thought Jolene. You need to tell somebody before this fool kills you."

I shook my head adamantly.

"He not gone kill me."

Nicole began to turn on the facet in the girl's bathroom and wet a paper towel. She began to pat my bruises with the cold napkin. I grimaced a little and welcomed the relief on my back.

"You don't know that Jolene. That man is crazy. I can't keep doing this." Nicole warned.

"Doing what?"

"Keeping your secret. It's eating me up on the inside."

"What do you think I should do?"

"The next time he put his hands on you call the police."

Chapter Twelve

Mr. Hightower was right I was failing school. It was hard for me to concentrate on school when I was responsible for looking out for my siblings. No matter how hard I tried to pretend like nothing was wrong with me. On the inside it felt like I was carrying everybody I loved on my shoulders and it was slowing me down. Quitting school seemed like the best thing to do. Mr. Hightower never called my parents because

I somehow convinced that I would try my best to bring my grades up.

I was a professional liar. I'd lied so much to everyone around me that I couldn't see the truth if it stood in front of me. It seemed like lying was easier than telling the truth. The truth was Melvin was selling dope out of the home. He'd lost both of his legs due to a rare disease in his blood. My momma worked most of the time to try to keep a roof over our heads and Melvin taken care. But I could tell that father time was not being kind to her anymore. She'd lost that special sparkle in her eyes from years ago.

She Kept Going Part 1 — Simmone Jones

Nowadays she'd just sit for five minutes in a corner stooped over the stove with red heavy eyes. I desperately wanted to save my mom and give her back the parts of herself that she'd freely given to others out of the kindness of her heart. Lord knows I prayed every night. My prayers went unanswered. Felt like God was more mad at me for complaining about my situation than I was about living. A some point I decided to just shut up and lie to keep from crying on the outside.

I was doing just that when Melvin pissed me off for the one last time. He called me everything from ugly to lazy. Nothing I ever did around the house could satisfy Melvin's needs. He was too demanding. He'd ask me to make him a ham and cheese sandwich with extra mayo. We were almost out of mayo, so I substituted the mayo with mustard and blue cheese dressing. I didn't think he would notice that much. Besides we were low on food and barely getting by with the little we had to survive.

I placed the ham and cheese sandwich on the kitchen table and walked upstairs. Melvin sat inside the living room and watched his favorite program. He was known for watching one of those court shows. He thought he could brush up on his legal jargon when the police got behind his tale.

"Sandwich is on the table." I uttered and walked rapidly up the stairs.

Melvin didn't even utter a thank you or look in my direction. Instead he just ignored me and kept staring at the television. I rolled my eyes and bit my bottom lip. It bothered me but I didn't want it to show on my face. I wasn't in my room five minutes getting ready to paint my toenails when I heard Melvin screaming my name.

"Jolene!" He exclaimed angrily.

My heart started beating rapidly inside my chest. I took a few deep breaths and made my way down the stairs. Each footstep was shorter than the last. I told myself that whatever Melvin had to say I'd let it roll off my shoulders. I stared Melvin in his big brown bulging eyes as he held the sandwich in the air. His crusted bottom lips and dry skin irritated my soul. Sometimes I just wanted to smack him upside his head with a bottle of Vaseline.

"Yes."

"Jolene, what kind of sandwich is this?" Melvin inquired.

I stuttered lightly as I selected my words. "It's a sandwich just like you told me to make it. "

"This ain't the damn sandwich I told you to make girl. Don't get smart at the mouth now. I'll still whip your butt from way over here."

I nod my head.

"This supposed to be mayo on the sandwich. Not some mess you done made up inside that crazy head of yours." Melvin retorted disgustedly.

I shrug my shoulders. "Ain't no more mayonnaise so what you want me to do?"

Melvin sucked his teeth and stared at his sandwich in disgust. He shook his head slowly and rolled his eyes in my direction. I didn't know what to expect next with Melvin. He began to rip the sandwich apart as if he was feeding pigeons at the park. One by one pieces of moist bread flew across the room in my direction.

"Stop!"

"You stupid enough to try to fool me with some fake mayo. Take your butt to the store and buy some." Melvin added.

More bread came flying in my direction as tears began to run down my face. Melvin began to laugh and taunt me.

"I don't have any money."

Melvin began to laugh harder as he started throwing pieces of meat in my direction from his wheelchair.

"Figure it out." Melvin warned.

Meat particles began to stick to my thick coils. I was so angry I wanted to kill Melvin and worry about the police later.

"I hate you! I wish that you were dead!!" I screamed.

It was like Melvin lost the little mind he had left inside in big head. He began to throw the remainder of the sandwich at me including the plate. I ran for cover upstairs in my bedroom. Luckily, I had the cordless phone inside my bedroom from earlier. I knew Melvin was going to kill me, so I need to protect myself from him as soon as possible.

"Hello 911.... I need to report an emergency."

When the police came, I chose to cover my bruises and sit far away from Melvin as possible. One female and one male officer showed up to house. The male officer stood inside the living room and talked to Melvin. After a few minutes of looking me over the female over escorted me into the bathroom. She helped wipe my eyes and asked me what was going on inside the home.

I didn't want to tell her the whole truth because I knew they would separate all of us. I wasn't crazy enough to trust a cop. I told her only the half truth about Melvin.

"Things go out of hand earlier because I didn't do what he wanted me to do." I admitted.

"What did he want you to do sweetie?"

"To go to the store and buy some mayo."

The officer looked at me like most adults look at teenagers. Like I was a problem and my parent or stepdad was the solution. She patted me on my shoulder and gave me some speech about listening to adults and staying out of trouble. I knew it was some bs. But I decided to let her have it for the sake of argument. When we returned to the living room Melvin and the male police officer were laughing like two old friends. I rolled my eyes in Melvin's direction.

"We're all good here right?" The male officer asked.

The female officer nodded her head and rubbed my back. "Yeah, we're good."

"Listen to your stepdad young lady. He's a good man and wouldn't tell you anything wrong. "The male officer warned.

I nodded my head and half smiled. When they left our home, Melvin made me go into my room without dinner. That night I cried my eyes out. I cried so much that it felt like my soul had left my body. I gazed up at the stars in the sky and wished that God would send me an angel. An angel that lived in Mississippi her name was Grandma Cookie.

Chapter Thirteen

A storm was coming. A storm unlike any other that I had seen before in my life. I could feel it down in my bones. I was tired. Too tired to focus on school or anything else in my life at the moment. I made the tough decision to drop out of school in the ninth grade.

It was either get kicked out or drop out. The things I was dealing with at home filled up my mind. I desperately wanted a normal life like the kids I went to school with on a daily. But the cards I'd been dealt in life were less than perfect. Everything was falling apart at home.

Some days we'd come in the house and the power would be shut off. Momma either would forget to pay the electric bill or she wouldn't have enough money to pay in full. When things like that happened, we lit candles around the house and made peanut butter and jelly sandwiches for dinner.

She Kept Going Part 1 — Simmone Jones

I watched my mom work her fingers down to the bone trying to provide for our household. Her efforts just weren't enough to keep us afloat for long periods of time. Melvin was a growing mole on all of our backs. He didn't help much around the house. He put us all in risk by selling drugs out the back door. No matter how many times my mother begged him to stop. He'd lie and say he just needed to sell enough to pay the rent that month. It was always something that needed to be paid. An argument that would leave me feeling more broken and confused on the inside than before in my life.

She Kept Going Part 1 — Simmone Jones

I was spiraling out of control. The only person I could confide in was my Grandma Cookie. I swear I was the spitting image of this woman. She walked with her head held high and back straight. Her tongue was just as sharp as her mind. She never bit her tongue for nobody on anything. She said life was too short to accept other people's bullshit.

When I told her that things around the house had caused me to drop out of school, she nearly had a heart attack.

"What you mean you dropped out?!" Grandma Cookie screamed through the phone.

"I needed to help momma around the house with the kids. I'll go back to school one day grandma." I insisted.

"That ain't right Jolene. "Grandma Cookie retorted. "You are a beautiful young woman with a bright future ahead of you. I refuse to let you become another statistic in this world, you hear me."

"Yes ma'am." I confirmed.

I knew Grandma Cookie meant every word coming out of her mouth. I'd spent a few summers in Mississippi with her and my relatives. Besides fattening me up most days Grandma Cookie and I had a special relationship. She'd talk to me about being a woman in this world. Not just any type of woman but a proud black woman. She'd tell me stories of her younger days and how all the men wanted to wife her. Grandma Cookie was never one for tradition. She did things on her accord not anybody else's. She lived her life that way and wanted nothing less for me.

When I mentioned the problems, I'd been having with Melvin she nearly crawled through the phone.

Grandma Cookie exploded into a pit of rage. She called Melvin every ungodly name in the book. A few names I couldn't even repeat or heard of before. Melvin tried his best to fight back with Grandma Cookie. But, his want to be gangster was no match for Grandma Cookie. Her words were law, and nobody could do anything about it.

A few weeks later the house grew eerily quiet. It was like Grandma Cookie had moved in with us and changed everything. Melvin wasn't bothering me as much anymore. I could tell by the look in my mother's eyes that she knew something was missing inside of me. Something that I'd lost within everything we'd been through in the last seven years. I didn't know exactly how to explain it. I just knew I needed to find that special part of myself again.

My mother sat me on the bed and hugged me like I was a newborn. I could feel her tears wetting my hair. I hugged her back in return. I knew she loved me and was sorry for all the pain she'd caused me over the years. I knew it would take some time for me to heal completely. Forgiveness was always easy for me. I needed to forgive myself first before I could forgive anyone else.

Through her tear stained eyes my mother said, "This came in the mail for you today."

I opened the letter and it was a bus ticket to Mississippi from Grandma Cookie. I didn't know exactly what to say or feel in the moment. Instead I just hugged my mom and told her I loved her no matter what. I could tell she was angry and felt as if I wasn't upfront with her, thank God she understood at least at this moment.

I was ready for a new chapter of my life to start in Mississippi….to be continued.

She Kept Going Part 1

Simmone Jones

What happens to the broken parts of us?

Growing up as a young girl in Georgia wasn't picture perfect for Jolene and her siblings. The daughter of a hard-working single mom dedicated to loving the wrong man. Jolene loses parts of herself overnight. Childhood traumas and tragic events cause an insurmountable pain for a young woman blossoming in the summer of 93. Forced to grow up in unpredictable circumstances, Jolene must make a difficult choice time and time again. Will she survive her difficult upbringing? Will she become another statistic?

Based on real life events, She Kept Going is a three-part series of a young woman's harrowing trials and tribulations to fight for the life she rightly deserved.

Made in the USA
Las Vegas, NV
30 September 2021